A Missionary Pictorial

The Ends of the Earth

W. Harold Fuller

2

Author: W. Harold Fuller
Production Manager: R. Donald Banks
Graphics Artist: Eric Read
Editorial Consultant: Kerry E. Lovering
Art Consultant: Charles J. Guth
Editorial Assistant: Rebecca J. Fuller
Distribution Manager: John Koop

Contributing Photographers (see page 95 for list of photograph credits):

Beth Black
Rodney Dixon
Barkley Fahnestock
Kenneth Fowler
Derek Frost
W. Harold Fuller

Donald Gale
Charles J. Guth
Kerry E. Lovering
Arnel Motz
James E. Plueddeman
Kenneth Radach

James Repperd
Donald Stilwell
Charles Truxton
Mark Wilson

A Missionary Pictorial

CONTENTS

Introduction   3
Foreword   4

THE ANDES
Overview   7
Religion and revolution   10
City dwellers   12
The white trail   17
Compassion: Combasé   19
The Word at work   20

AFRICA
Overview   23
The nations   25
The restless ones   26
The call of many voices   32
Islam   37
Message of life   40
Search for knowledge   43
Away from the restive crowds   46
The habitants   52
A season for everything   56
Sharing with people God loves   62
Tradition   64
Cattle and culture   66
Famine   69
Helping people help themselves   78
Healing in Jesus' Name   80
The Church at work   82
Partakers of His sufferings   86
New frontiers   90
Doing what Jesus told us   94
Photograph credits   94

COVER PHOTOGRAPHS
Front and back: A sure foot and strong lungs are needed on the trail high in the Andes Mountains.
Inside front: An Indian farmer and his family eke out a precarious living on the spine of an Andean ridge.
Inside back: The African countryside grows hushed in the path of a rolling tropical storm.

© SIM International 1983
First published 1983
All rights reserved
No portion of this book may be reproduced in any form without written permission from the publisher
ISBN 0 919470 08 4
Library of Congress Catalogue: Card No. 83 50482

3

"You shall be witnesses unto me . . .
unto the uttermost part of the earth."
Jesus Christ, Lord and Saviour

FORWARD IN THE *POSSIBLE* TASK

Jesus Christ did not give His church an impossible task. When He commanded us to bear witness to "the ends of the earth," He also gave us the power to do it. He gave us His Holy Spirit.

I have been privileged to see personally how that power is at work through SIM missionaries and national Christians in Africa and Latin America.

SIM began with a vision shared by very few people. Many thought the vision was just a dream, an unrealistic concept of evangelizing unreached people in far-off places. The founders of SIM, and their followers, were people of faith and vision who were convinced of God's purposes for them as well as for Africa and Latin America. Their vision did not become a reality easily. The difficulties were great, but they persevered. We give thanks to God for His faithful working in and through their lives.

But we don't live in the past. That would be dangerous. It would be the first step toward becoming archaic – to allowing the rust of antiquity to weaken us and make us unable to cope with today's world. We live *now*, not *then* – in a vastly different world from the days of our founders.

We must learn from the past and give thanks for our fathers. Having done that, we must seek to apply their principles to our day. With gratitude to God we now see the impossible dream coming true as His church is being raised up.

This book tells today's story. It is a different kind of missionary report. It depends mainly on photographs. I have walked many of the trails, looked across the ranges, and been gripped by the scenes pictured here. Now I am delighted that you too can see for yourself God at work through His servants.

You will also see why missionaries love their work – why they have true joy in service. And why not? What greater commission could anyone have than to stand in Christ's stead beseeching people to be reconciled to God?

My hope is that through this book you will rejoice with those who rejoice in their service for God – and then pray for them. Find joy in service yourself as, led by the Holy Spirit, you share with them through prayer.

Ian M. Hay

Ian M. Hay
General Director
SIM

Foreword

As an editor, I've put together many photographic features. But this is the most unusual I have ever worked on.

Ideally an editor starts with a theme, and then assigns his photographers. In this case, we asked several missionaries to send us a selection of photographs. Out of two thousand pictures, we narrowed down the selection to the 136 (plus two maps) you see in this book.

I am astounded by what has emerged: a multi-imaged record of real life – the people and events surrounding our missionaries as they've been busy taking the gospel to "the ends of the earth."

We've purposely added very few words, for if "a photo is worth ten thousand words," we don't need to add more than a brief explanation here and there. Many of the photos speak volumes, and so we hope you will take the time to absorb what they say so graphically.

Because we limited ourselves to photos already taken and available, it was impossible to represent comprehensively any country or people or ministry. For that reason we have not named places or people. If we had begun to do so, there are many whose names and faces should have been included; instead they and their ministries are represented simply by those who happened to be on the spot when the missionary photographer clicked the shutter.

Although the photographs were taken in only two continents, and only parts of them, we believe that they represent the way the Holy Spirit is working around our globe through the many agencies of the gospel.

We do not want to imply that *we* live in the favoured center of the world, and everyone else lives in exotic "far corners." After all, our own lands are part of "the ends of the earth" to which our Lord referred when He commissioned His disciples in Jerusalem. Africa and South America are closer to Jerusalem than some of the other far-flung lands from which SIM missionaries come. Today they join hands with believers in Africa and the Andes, helping God's people around the world fulfill Christ's assignment: "to the ends of the earth."

I know the missionary photographers' hearts were stirred as they recorded life around them. Mine has been challenged as I have pored over the photos in putting this book together. I pray that your heart too will rejoice in God's creation, reach out in love to people Christ died for, and gladly respond to whatever God tells you to do.

W. Harold Fuller

W. Harold Fuller

4

"He shall speak peace unto the heathen;
and his dominion shall be from sea even to sea,
and from the river even to *the ends of the earth.*

Zechariah 9:10

THE ANDES

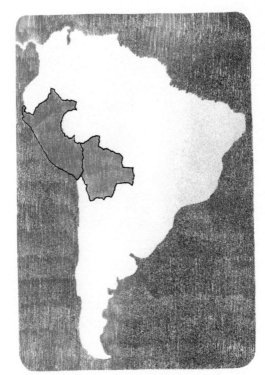

Stretching over 5,000 miles from north to south and rising above 22,000 feet, the Andes Mountains form the spine of South America's West. The area of SIM responsibility is Peru and Bolivia, which countries straddle the middle section of the range.

Climate varies all the way from the Peruvian coast, where rain has not fallen for 25 years, to the rarified atmosphere of grazing land 12,000 feet above sea level, down to the steamy rain forests of the Amazon tributaries on the eastern side.

Main language groups are the Quechua and Aymara Indians, who formed the core of the ancient Inca empire. Industrious and organized, the Incas grew crops on the mountain slopes while mining silver and gold deep inside them. Lust for the precious metals brought the Spaniards, who conquered the empire in the 1530s and left their own culture and progeny behind when their government was overthrown by an Indian uprising led by Simon Bolivar in the 19th century.

Bolivia and Peru have since struggled through successive revolutions – Bolivia having had 190 governments in 156 years. Present economic conditions, with inflation topping 300% at times, add to the political problems of the two nations, South America's poorest.

The sun god was the main deity of the Incas, and pagan rites still continue alongside the Roman Catholicism introduced by the Spaniards. Peru and Bolivia are officially more than 90% Roman Catholic. The spiritual emptiness of the people provides an unparalleled opportunity for the gospel.

The ministry for which SIM is now responsible began in 1907 as the Bolivian Indian Mission, founded by New Zealander George Allan. He took the gospel into Bolivia by mule, over trails such as shown in our cover photo. Renamed the Andes Evangelical Mission when it spread into Peru, the mission later approached SIM to consider a merger, and in 1982 became the Andes Area of SIM. The mission works closely with other evangelical agencies in the two countries, jointly channelling converts into an indigenous church association in each country. These total around 1200 congregations.

SIM's strategy in the Andes Area is to continue seeking out unreached peoples, whether in remote villages high on the *altiplano* or in sub-cultures of the city ghettos, or in the new lowland settlements. While doing so, SIM also helps to meet the physical needs of people hit by both drought and flood, ministering to the whole man.

Burdened for unreached peoples, the churches have asked SIM to help them develop a program of mobilizing and equipping believers to witness to all in their own communities, as well as to send out teams to other unreached peoples. This calls for sacrificial commitment and courage in the midst of unsettled and difficult conditions.

Llama, raised for their wool and meat, roam the hillsides.

Opposite: Descendant of the Inca Empire, a Christian girl wears a colorful blanket hand-woven on local looms. *Top:* Perched on a mountain pinnacle, ancient ruins of Machu Picchu give hints of the skills of an earlier civilization in the Andes Mountains. *Below:* Andean terrace farming methods (distant slope) introduced by the Incas, and work in mining towns (foreground). It was the Incas' silver and gold which brought the Spanish invaders and led to the overthrow of the Empire.

RELIGION AND REVOLUTION

Right: An historic monument commemorating women who defended their city combines the deep religious and patriotic feelings of the people. The Indian sun worshippers took Roman Catholic externals from the Spanish. Ever since the overthrow of the Spaniards, they have lived through successive coups and revolutions. Now new forces press on them, as shown by the Communist hammer and sickle painted on the wall of a cathedral (*below*). Squatting woman pays a man to say her prayers for her professionally. Incense candles on the sidewalk are for praying to the saints.

Left: A teacher hopes that this crucifix on the wall of his one-room abode will ensure protection and prosperity. *Below:* A devil mask epitomizes the fear many have of evil spirits.

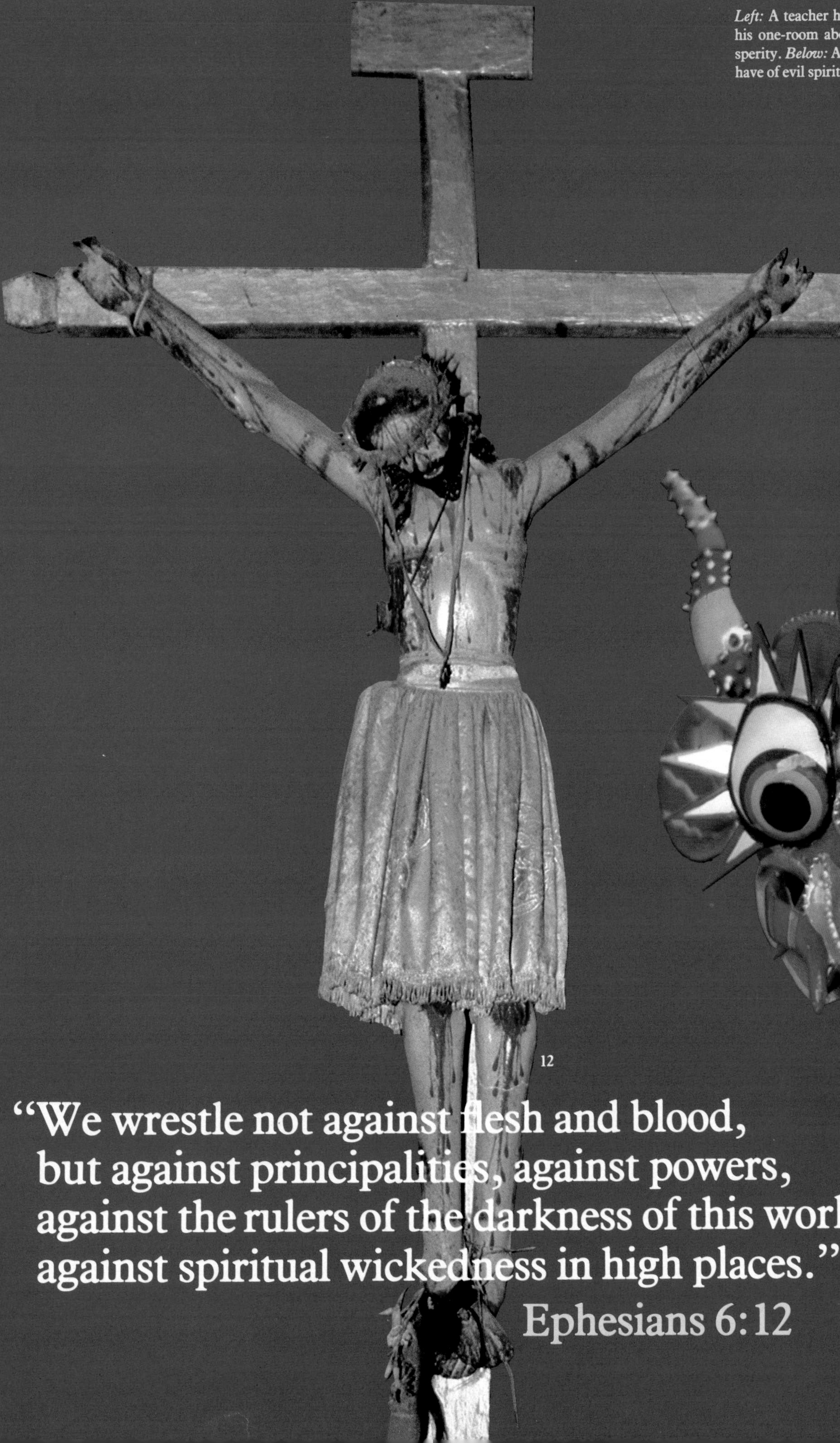

12

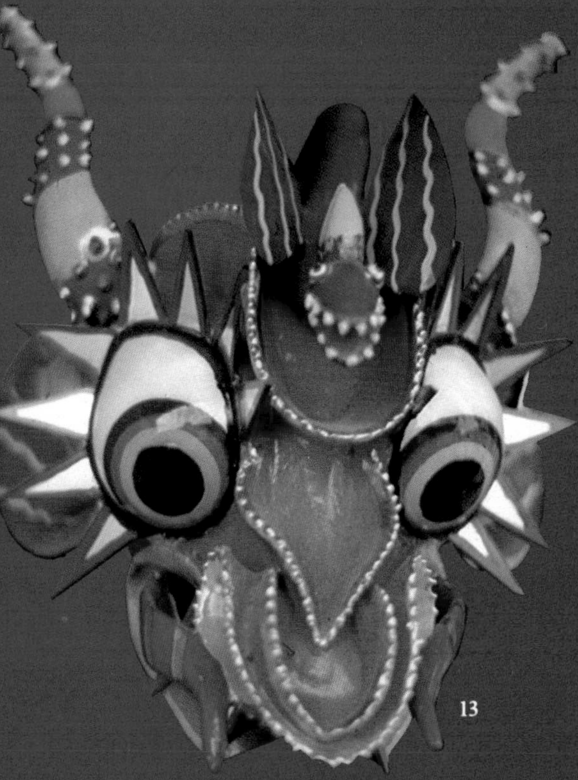

13

"We wrestle not against flesh and blood,
but against principalities, against powers,
against the rulers of the darkness of this world,
against spiritual wickedness in high places."

Ephesians 6:12

CITY DWELLERS

While the affluent live in high rise suites *(below)*, others crowd into hovels *(bottom)* as the population continues to stream into the cities in search of employment.

14

15

16

17

Top: A vegetable vendor hopes to sell to pedestrians, who stride past grumbling at ever rising prices. *Below:* A herbalist proclaims the reputed healing properties of his medicines.

Top: Unemployed youths anxiously scan the jobs list being chalked on a board outside an employment agency. *Below:* An anxious mother pushes through the market place, concerned about providing food for her family.

A meaningless cycle for people without Christ, life's journey may end in a burial wall. On All Souls Day relatives say special prayers and decorate the vaults with flowers.

"All our days are passed away in thy wrath, we spend our years as a tale that is told."

Psalm 90:9

THE WHITE TRAIL

For many cocaine "snorters" in the rest of the world, the white powdery trail begins back on the humid lowlands in the shadow of the Andes, where the coca plant grows profusely. Struggling families *(below)* can make ten times what they would earn from growing other crops. Christians face an ethical problem, knowing that although there is a legitimate medical market, most coca is either chewed or made into cocaine, leaving a trail of destruction. *Bottom:* The tension became so great for this pastor and family that they fled the area despite loss of support. A missionary encourages them in their faith.

22

23

17

21

24

Whether river dwellers in the lowlands or farmers of the *altiplano* (high plain), destitute people find hope in the gospel. *Top:* The SIM, along with other agencies, was able to rush aid to flooded tributaries of the Amazon, where dugout canoes like this one are the main mode of transport. *Right:* A church-planting missionary introduces a farmer to hybrid seed which will increase his harvest – and come to fruition earlier. *Below:* Sugar cane is a staple cash crop but has suffered from depressed world prices.

26

25

18

COMPASSION IS SPELLED COMBASÉ

27

28

SIM works with other evangelical agencies through a joint relief and development organization, COMBASÉ. *Above:* a mother waits for her children to be attended at a COMBASÉ clinic. *Left:* Meeting spiritual needs is central to the whole program. An evangelist explains the way of salvation to an Indian miner, whose cheek bulges with coca leaves (chewed like tobacco).

"Jesus . . . was moved with compassion toward them, because they were as sheep not having a shepherd."

Mark 6:35

THE WORD AT WORK

"Faith comes by hearing, and hearing by the Word of God." – Romans 10:17. Soldiers listen attentively to the preaching of a national missionary *(inset)*.

32

33

Above: Quechua believers happily line up for the inevitable "group photo" – but this time on top of the world – at the ends of the earth. Across the Andean ridges countless other Indians still wait to be told the Good News in their own tongue. *Left:* Spiritual "shepherd" for several "flocks," this Indian evangelist has studied the Scriptures through the extension (TEE) method, used by missionaries. He has a vision to reach others. *Opposite page (bottom):* Preparing for leadership, seminary students compare notes with their principal (on the right of the picture) and a visiting missionary.

"All the ends of the world shall . . .
turn unto the Lord; and all the kindreds of the nations
shall worship before Thee."

Psalm 22:27

Mysterious link between Africa and South America, reed canoes used on isolated lake in the African interior are also found on a remote lake high in the Andes Mountains.

AFRICA

One-fifth of the world's land surface, the African continent is home to one out of every ten earthlings, with over two thousand languages among fifty-three nations. The photos in this section cover SIM's area of responsibility, in a broad swath four thousand miles across the widest part of Africa.

Until the 18th and 19th centuries' explorations opened up trade and travel, the vast continent was largely unknown to her own peoples and to the rest of the world. "Timbuctu," at the end of the caravan route across the Sahara, became synonymous for "the ends of the earth." Towards the end of the last century European powers competed to set up spheres of influence, drawing political lines around their colonies – boundaries zealously preserved by today's independent states.

With the passing of the colonial era, Communist ideology has sought to gain its own sphere of influence. While some states are Marxist today, their brand is mainly nationalist socialism; above all, African states are fervently independent, refusing to be dominated by new ideological lords in place of the former colonial masters.

While much African life may have superficial similarities because of climate and geography, actually ethnic groups even within the same nation may vary vastly in culture. Our photos show customs in some groups which may be unheard of in others.

Famine, refugee problems, spiralling inflation, and the world's highest birth rates have hit Africa hard economically. High oil prices brought boom times to African oil-producing states for a decade but sent other states diving into debt – some must borrow more, simply to pay the interest on old debts.

For centuries the Sahara formed a barrier to Islam's southward spread. As the sea routes opened up, the gospel penetrated from the coasts further south. Today Islam and Chritianity compete for first place as Africa's number one religion. One research predicts that by the turn of this century Christianity will be the majority religion – that is, there will be more Christians than Muslims. However, statistics of the phenomenal increase of Christians (one estimate: 16,000 per day) chiefly represent the rapidly expanding birth rate in ethnic groups termed "Christian". Adults who do take on the name "Christian," mostly from animist (pagan) religions, include every known sect as well as nominal Christianity.

While the number of true conversions in some tribes is a matter for thanksgiving, the sobering fact is that there are millions in other tribes who, because of linguistic and cultural barriers, have not yet heard that Christ died for them.

SIM pioneers first entered Africa in 1893. Discouragement, disease, and death did not deter them and others from taking the gospel to unreached people. SIM continues to pioneer with church-planting teams. The mission also works in partnership with the indigenous churches which have sprung up from its ministry in Benin, Ethiopia, Ghana, Ivory Coast, Liberia, Niger, Nigeria, Sudan, and Upper Volta. These total around five thousand congregations with approximately two million adherents. SIM shares its facilities, such as radio, with other evangelical missions, and works closely with them in joint projects – as in Kenya, where SIM assists in Somali outreach and other projects on behalf of the Africa Inland Mission and its churches.

In pursuing its one great objective of bringing people to the Saviour, SIM also demonstrates Christ's love by meeting physical need. The following pages show Spirit-empowered men and women letting God use a wide range of skills to do what Christ told His disciples: *to be His witnesses to the ends of the earth.*

THE NATIONS

Typifying the emergence of nearly fifty independent states since the Fifties, a standard bearer (*left*) raises the flag of his nation, while soldiers proudly march past (*below*). African states meet under the colorful window mural (*bottom*) of the Organization of African Unity to grapple with the colossal problems of poverty, illiteracy, and tensions which erupt periodically in violence and war.

36

37

5

THE RESTLESS ONES . . . stream into the cities

Previous and opposite pages: Uprooted from their traditional rural ways, Africa's youth stream into the cities, circling high-rise commercial buildings *(top)* with squalid shanty towns *(bottom).*

Women stop to admire modern fashions on a mannequin *(left),* but they'll do most of their shopping in the traditional market place *(below),* where prices are lower.

29

"The Gentiles (nations) shall come unto you from *the ends of the earth*, and shall say, Surely our fathers have inherited lies, vanity, and things wherein there is no profit."

Jeremiah 16:19

The sophisticated find time and place for leisurely enjoyment, while for the sweating "street boys" happiness is "a drag on a joint" – but all can find true satisfaction only through reconciliation with God. Africa's rapid urbanization provides a strategic opportunity for gospel outreach.

45

THE CALL OF MANY VOICES

Opposite page: The electronic age has brought a modern babel of voices to Africa, luring people through radio and cassette tapes. Status symbol for aspiring youth, the tape recorder has potential for good and evil. These youths are intent on recording music at an outdoor gathering.

Ideologies such as Communism (*left*) have been quick to use radio and literature to get their message across to Africa's "restless ones." *Below:* Sects from around the world are making an impact on people in a continent looking for new answers to problems old and new.

Above: Traditional religion, largely spirit worship, provides a tie with the past for people surrounded by change. Here masqueraders representing ancestors lead a festival to placate the spirits and invoke prosperity.
Right: Fetish priests (witch doctors) wield enormous power among followers filled with fear of witchcraft.
Left: Judaism and medieval Christianity combine in the ancient rites of the Ethiopian Orthodox Church. Throughout the continent the trappings of nominal Christianity often are a veneer over deep-seated pagan beliefs. Sects with a mixture of Christian and pagan elements grow rapidly, promising a new formula of magic to solve daily problems.

ISLAM

The most extensive influence in Africa of any non-Christian system, religious or secular, is the Muslim religion, Islam. Currently numbering over 200 million in the continent, or 41% of the population, Muslims vary from orthodox Arabs of North Africa to syncretistic blacks further south. Islam is a complete life-system, influencing every aspect of life. Muslim salvation is based on good works and ritual, such as the Friday "sallah" prayer gathering shown here. Yet there can be no assurance of salvation, for there is no living Saviour.

52

Above: This elderly Muslim was taught as a boy to recite lengthy passages of the Muslim's holy book, the Koran. He wears amulets inscribed with its words, and daily he repeats its passages. His mind conditioned to accept things by rote rather than by reason, he is blind in spiritual understanding. But God loves him, and he needs someone to show him God's love. *Right:* A member of a nomadic Muslim tribe reads the Gospel of John for the first time. Translated by SIM linguists and written in the world's oldest living script, Shifina, it is the living Word empowered by the Holy Spirit to open eyes spiritually.

Veteran pioneer, warmly accepted by Saharan nomads because of his love for them, here points the way to the living Saviour.

"Look unto me, and be ye saved, all *the ends of the earth*; for I am God, and there is none else."
Isaiah 45:22

"Their sound went into all the earth,
and their words unto *the ends of the world.*"
Romans 10:18

MESSAGE OF LIFE

The message of eternal life breaks through the confusion of voices calling out to Africa today. The people hear it in their own language and in their own familiar context of life. SIM's Radio ELWA beams out the message forty transmitter hours daily in 45 languages, right across the continent. By radio and cassette tapes, technicians and producers *(right)* speed the message to every spectrum of life – including the modern business woman *(below)*. The message also penetrates the mud walls of Muslim compounds, otherwise closed to messengers of the gospel *(bottom)*.

57

58

59

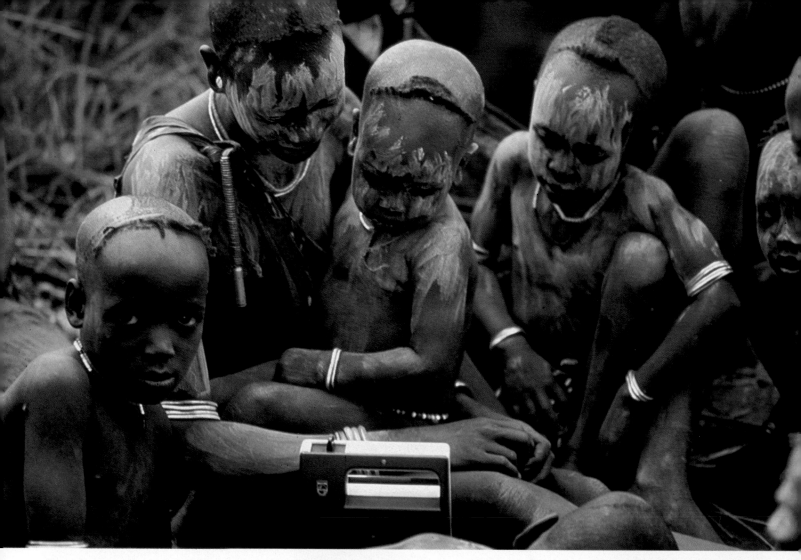

Above: A rural family huddles around a cassette tape player to hear in their own language that Jesus died for them, while urban readers *(right)* scan the shelves of a Christian bookshop for books that will help them face their changing world. ECWA Productions Ltd. has a network of 38 bookshops. Challenge Enterprises of Ghana has a mobile gospel film and literature ministry.

SEARCH FOR KNOWLEDGE

As people become literate, many look upon education as the solution to all problems. Expectations rise and governments are hard pressed to meet the demand for studies at every level.

50   62

51   63

Open, enquiring minds are eager to absorb anything, including the teacher's life-style. The tragedy is the influence of godless teachers. The challenge is the opportunity for Christians to teach everything from the arts *(below)* to Bible Knowledge, on the curriculum in several countries.

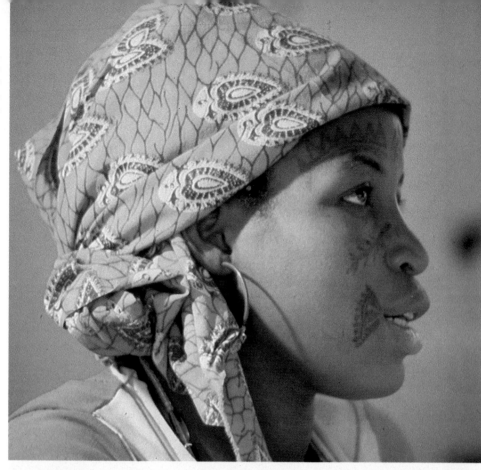

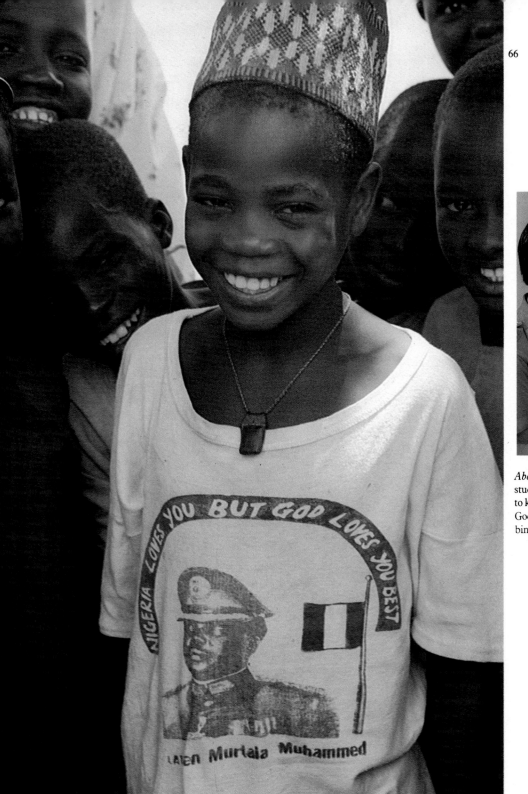

Above: Missionary teachers enjoy personal contact with students during and after school hours, leading students to know the grand objective of all knowledge: the love of God, who gave His only Son. *Left:* A schoolboy combines patriotism and Christian witness.

"The fear of the Lord is the beginning of wisdom,
a good understanding
have all they that do His commandments."
Psalm 111:10

AWAY FROM THE RESTIVE CROWDS

68

Displaying the beauty of God's creation and reminding us of His care, a tiny malachite kingfisher balances on a grass stalk, while wide-winged pelicans gracefully settle by a lake.

"You are worthy, O Lord,
to receive glory and honour and power,
for you have created all things,
and for thy pleasure
they are and were created."

Revelation 4:11

72

73

74

Lions, rhinos, and giraffes are part of Africa's splendid wildlife heritage. *Top:* Baboons may be fun to watch but they are unpopular with farmers whose crops they raid. *Previous pages:* A bull elephant protects his herd crossing the trail.

THE HABITANTS

Far from the turmoil of the cities, many African families live in quiet clusters of huts which blend in with their farms and the landscape.

"Bring my sons from far,
and my daughters from *the ends of the earth*."
Isaiah 43:6

A time to work...

"To everything there is a season,
and a time to every purpose under the heaven."
Ecclesiastes 3:1,2

Women winnow and pound grain in mortars, preparing for the main meal of the day.

57

. . . and a time to dance

Young women take part in a traditional dance involving spirit worship. In pagan religions, a birth or death, a farewell or homecoming, the erection of a hut or digging of a well, the planting of seed or harvesting of crops – all call for sacrifice to the spirits accompanied with dancing.

...a time to plant and to harvest

In a labor-intensive rural society, the farmers have hand plowed (with hoes) this entire field. Mechanization would only add exorbitant fuel costs and create problems of maintenance.

. . . and a time to fish

In some communities, the annual fishing festival is the highlight of the year. A large pool in the river is blocked off by nets, and at a given signal brawny fishermen plunge in to see who can capture the largest fish by net, spear, or hand! Enormous Nile Perch are the winning trophies – some weighing over 300 pounds.

Sharing with people God loves

Below: Sharing the Word of God in their own home – a missionary visits with a village family, listening to a gospel message taped in their own tongue. *Opposite page:* Walking with the people along the paths they trudge – praying that some might accept The Way.

82

62

"I have set you to be a light of the Gentiles,
that you should be for salvation unto *the ends of the earth.*"
Acts 13:47

83

TRADITION

Africa proudly retains many of her ancient traditions, keeping the people in touch with their ancestral roots.

85

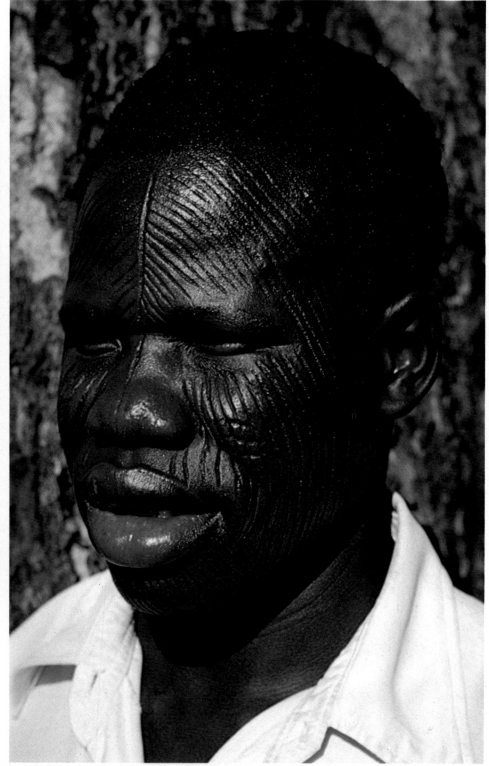

86

Left: A personable young woman in an isolated village obviously enjoys the mud-pack hair style of her people. *Above:* This famous Benin bronze, dating back at least a thousand years, lends antiquity to the tradition of facial markings *(right)*. Now performed only occasionally in a few cultures, the custom likely arose to identify people in case they were carried off during inter-tribal warfare. Today adults with tribal markings are proud of this instant recognition of their ancestry.

"God has made of one blood all nations of men . . .
and has determined the times before appointed
and the bounds of their habitation,
that they should seek the Lord."

Acts 17:24

65

CATTLE AND CULTURE

Cattle are central to many nomadic societies, not only representing material wealth but also spirit kinship between tribe members. Cattle figure in celebrations of birth, puberty, marriage, and death. *Below:* A betrothed woman and relatives lead the prize bull of their herd, mammoth horns bedecked, around the village to announce the forthcoming wedding.

Opposite page: In a tribe that depends on cattle blood rather than meat for protein, young boys take turns drinking the blood from the neck of a calf they have lanced. They would not look upon this as cruelty, believing they have a spirit kinship with the calf.

Left: In another nomadic tribe, an evangelist opens the Word of God and plays a gospel tape for cattle herders. Extensive drought and cattle disease have made these proud, suspicious nomads more open to listening to the gospel as Christians have shown them God's love. Every household in one area became open to an SIM veterinarian who vaccinated the herdsmen's cattle against a devastating rinderpest epidemic – one day she vaccinated more than three thousand cattle!

88

FAMINE

"I was thirsty..."

As rains fail, the water table sinks, and livestock destroy the remaining scant foliage, herdsmen travel increasing distances to find precious water for their animals. The encroaching desert in many parts of Africa is the result of both natural and human problems involving millions of people. Woven grass containers in foreground are lined with red pitch, and are used for camel's milk or water. Cradled in wicker baskets, they travel for miles slung around a camel's hump.

"...and you gave me drink"

92

94

Providing a safe water supply may involve well-drilling, damming, or capping a formerly contaminated spring. SIM relief and development teams seek to avoid making communities reliant on imported equipment or costly fuel. *Above:* A team installs a pump made entirely from local materials. Designed by an SIM missionary, it is now widely used by the United Nations (UNICEF) water program. *Right:* Thirsty man drinks from a goat-skin "bucket". *Below:* A grateful woman fills her water pot with life-sustaining water.

93

95

"Ho, everyone that thirsts, come to the waters,
and he that has no money; come, buy, and eat;
yes, come, buy wine and milk
without money and without price."

Isaiah 55:1

"I was hungry..."

Problems of a rapidly growing population, cash crops replacing food crops, and sometimes counterproductive farming customs have been compounded by drought conditions – resulting in an estimated 20 million people in Africa going to bed hungry. Millions of those face starvation. Malnourished children are unable to convert vegetable protein as easily as adults, and are left susceptible to disease.

Left: Vultures in a dead tree keep a death watch.
Below: Searching for food and water, two men try to escape the searing sun beneath a thorn branch shelter.
Right: An emaciated mother suffering from tuberculosis, brings her dying child to the missionary, her last hope.

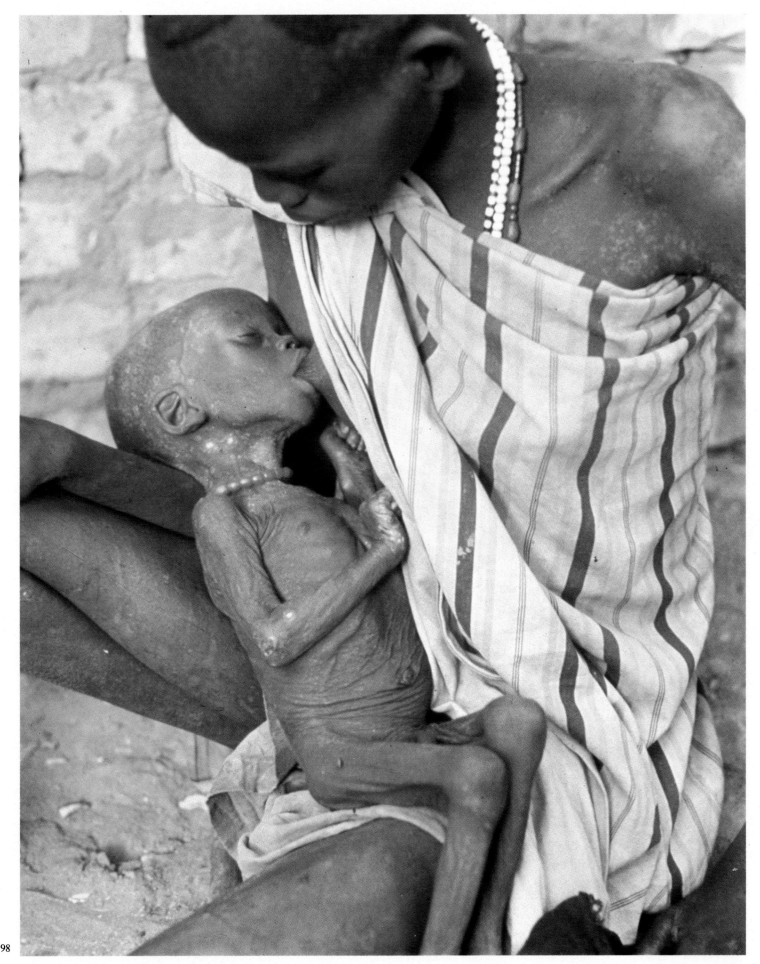

"..and you fed me"

Through its own relief department as well as in partnership with evangelical relief agencies, SIM rushes aid to meet emergency conditions. When evangelists reported crop failure in one area affecting five million people, the mission alerted other agencies and flew in supplies to help stave off starvation until other organizations could move in. *Left:* A desperate father brings his starving child to the mission relief center. *Right:* A hungry child, one-half his proper weight, gulps water while waiting in the food line. *Below:* A mother gratefully receives her ration of grain to feed the family.

100

101

HELPING PEOPLE
HELP THEMSELVES

Doling out food to hungry people looks like a simple solution for refugees or drought victims. But experience has shown that people soon become reliant on outside help and end up with greater problems. While emergency help is sometimes necessary, SIM believes the better way is to help people grow more food and care for their own needs. And while meeting physical need the mission also seeks to meet spiritual needs, so that not just the body but the whole man may find relief.

Right: Hybrid maize and other improved crops make better use of deteriorating soil and climate. *Opposite and below:* Missionary agriculturalists teach improved farming methods – while also planting the Good Seed of the Gospel.

103

104

02

HEALING IN JESUS NAME

Left: A young mother lovingly holds her sick child as a missionary nurse listens with her stethoscope on the child's back. *Below:* Valiant nurses make do under a grass shelter as they treat a stream of patients in an isolated village affected by an epidemic.

Medical work ranges from village health projects *(right)* to surgery in mission hospitals *(bottom).* But the desired result, healing for both body and soul, shows in the happy smile of a patient talking with the hospital evangelist *(below).*

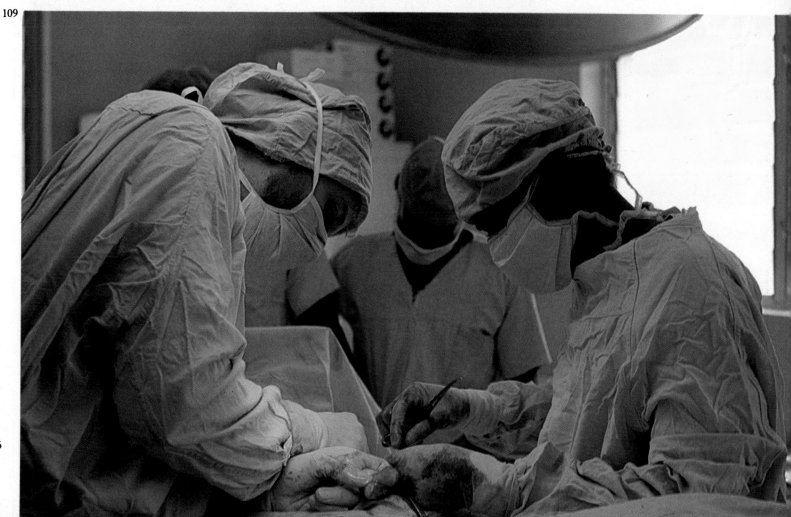

"Go into all the world . . .
and lo I am with you always,
even unto the end of the world."
Matthew 28:20

82

THE CHURCH AT WORK
to the
ends of the earth

Opposite: A rural Bible school, now entirely run by the local church, perches on top of a hill 9,000 feet above sea level. *Below:* Rural believers rejoice as they leave their Sunday worship service. *Right:* Despite local scarcity of water, a new believer witnesses to her faith through the act of baptism. *Bottom:* Christian youth join in an evangelistic crusade in a large city. The clenched fist salute is their culture's traditional gesture of honor shown to a chief – in this case the Lord of lords.

111

112

113

"According to thy name, O God, so is thy praise unto *the ends of the earth*."

Psalm 48:10

Bible study and praise deepen the life of the church. *Right:* A man and his daughter study the Word. *Below:* Women provide a soft percussive accompaniment to their singing by rhythmically cupping their hands over empty water pots.

114

115

Vital to the growth of the church is leadership preparation, from evangelism training in the vernacular right up to theological degree level. *Top:* Bible school student prepares himself in the Scriptures. *Bottom:* A teacher trained in the Word helps introduce the oncoming generation to the Saviour.

"…able to teach others also"
2 Timothy 2:2

PARTAKERS
OF HIS SUFFERINGS"

"As you are partakers of the sufferings,
so shall you be also of the consolation."
2 Corinthians 1:7

"I suffer trouble, as an evildoer, even unto bonds..."

These hands represent men and women whose photos we could have used. They also represent thousands of others who have never been photographed.

They stand for the suffering church.

While there is unprecedented liberty for the gospel in many parts of Africa, there are also places where God's people are persecuted – where evil forces would snuff out the church.

We personally know some of those who are in prison today, or who have lost family and property for the sake of their Saviour. We know students who have endured beatings rather than deny their faith. We know of pastors who have walked to their death in a mass grave. There have been more martyrs of the Cross in Africa this century than in any previous century.

To represent the suffering church, we decided not to use an individual's photo. For one thing, publicity could make things even more difficult. Moreover, those who suffer ask only that Jesus be glorified.

"Don't feel sorry for us," they've told us. "God is sifting His people and has privileged us to suffer for His name. Besides, He's giving us opportunity to witness for Him right here in prison."

So rather than single out a man or woman, we decided to represent the suffering church in Africa with a pair of hands lifted up in service and dedication. The hands are dusty and worn from much labor, but they are beautiful in the sight of the One who will say: "Well done, good and faithful servant;...enter into the joy of your Lord."

118
119

"... but the Word of God is not bound"
2 Timothy 2:9

Right: An evangelist from a land in which many believers lost their lives during a time of national persecution, continues to preach the message of freedom from sin.

Left: The commission given by Jesus to His disciples is boldly displayed on the door of a car used by the missionary arm of one of the churches which has grown from SIM's church-planting ministry. *Below:* An evangelist declares Jesus as Saviour to a group gathered under a tree.

"GO TO THE WHOLE WORLD AND PREACH THE GOSPEL TO ALL MANKIND."

KU TAFI KO INA CIKIN DUNIYA YI WA DUKKAN YAN ADAM BISHARA"

MARK 16:15.

120

121

122

88

"All *the ends of the earth* shall see the salvation of our God."

Isaiah 52:10

The goal of church planting is not simply an established church, but a body of believers who will be concerned for the unsaved around them and will in turn reach out to others. Here a national missionary teaches God's Word to a group of interested villagers. One man is recording the message, so others may hear it after the missionary has left.

123

NEW FRONTIERS

Other peoples wait for the Good News. *Left:* In one remote village, the chief challenged the missionary: "If this story of a Saviour is true, why haven't you come to tell us before now?" *Bottom:* Aided by an interpreter, a missionary tells the way of salvation to an unreached tribal group. *Below:* "We've tried other religions," the people said. "Now we want to know about this Jesus."

127

128

129

Above: This is a local church – so new the believers meet under a tree; they haven't had time to put up a building. Saved from pagan spirit worship, they now worship the living God. Such pioneer church planting is accomplished by living Christ among the people *(left)*, discipling believers in the Word *(lower left)*, and travailing in much prayer *(below)*.

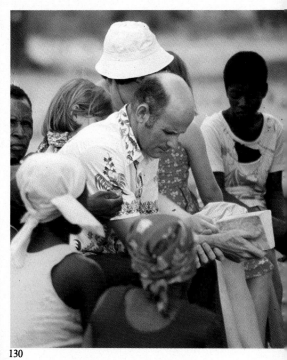

130

91

"The harvest is past,
 the summer is ended, and we are not saved."
Jeremiah 8:20

131

132

DOING WHAT JESUS TOLD US

Jesus Christ said to do it – and this missionary pictorial shows how His disciples are doing it today: meeting with new believers under the trees, training leadership to teach the Word, healing the sick, feeding the hungry, reaching new frontiers, confronting the very forces of hell.

But that's only part of it. To complete the picture, we'd have to add another section showing how disciples such as you all over our globe are making this possible.

It would never happen if people like you were not battling the forces of darkness in prayer.

You wouldn't have seen photos of people reaching people if men and women hadn't responded to Christ's commands and joined us in the staggering task.

These photos wouldn't have shown needy people receiving help if you had not given sacrificially.

But you've also had a glimpse of men, women, and children who still need to hear – who still wait for someone to go to the ends of the earth to tell them. We know where they are and who they are, but apart from the prayerful backing of God's people we'll never reach them before they face God's eternal judgment.

Current projections to meet the commitments we feel God wants us to undertake in the coming decade will require a 7% increase in recruits each year plus financial support for them and their ministries. This is not a random target, but represents carefully researched strategic tasks now waiting to be done. In faith we've accepted that assignment as our part in doing what Christ told us to do – be His witnesses to the ends of the earth. We need men and women of faith to help us do what Jesus told us to.

For up-to-date prayer requests or for information about urgent personnel and project needs, please write your nearest office:

AUSTRALIA: SIM, P.O. Box 171, Summer Hill, NSW 2130
CANADA: SIM, 10 Huntingdale Blvd., Scarborough, Ontario M1W 2S5
GREAT BRITAIN: SIM, 84 Beulah Hill, London SE19 3EP, England
NEW ZEALAND: SIM, P.O. Box 38588, Howick
SINGAPORE: SIM, Bras Basah, P.O. Box 239, Singapore 9118
SOUTHERN AFRICA: SIM, Box 64075, Highlands North, Johannesburg
SWITZERLAND: Société Internationale Missionnaire,
Rue de Genève 77 bis 1004 Lausanne
UNITED STATES: SIM, Cedar Grove, New Jersey 07009

PHOTOGRAPH CREDITS

(Photographs are numbered consecutively throughout the book.
Each of the following numbers refers to a photograph, not a page number.)

Beth Black: 51, 98, 106
Rodney Dixon: 38, 39, 45, 54, 64, 83, 93, 124, 125, 126, 131, 128, 129, 130, 133
Barkley Fahnestock: 35, 36, 60, 77, 82, 84, 87, 111, 116
Kenneth Fowler: 2, 8, 21, 90, 105
Derek Frost: 40, 43, 53, 61, 63, 72, 73, 79, 107, 108, 109, 134
W. Harold Fuller: 6, 7, 9, 10, 11, 15, 18, 19, 22, 23, 29, 31, 33, 34, 37, 42, 47, 48, 49, 50, 52, 55, 56, 59, 62, 65, 66, 71, 76, 78, 85, 86, 96, 105, 110, 112, 114, 119, 120, 121, 122, 131, 132
Donald Gale: 32

Charles J. Guth: 12, 13, 17, 20, 25, 27, 30
Kerry E. Lovering: 80
Arnel Motz: 1, 14, 16, 24, 26, 28
James E. Plueddemann: 113
Kenneth Radach: 89, 100
James Repperd: 4
Donald Stilwell: 3, 68, 69, 70, 75, 91, 92, 94, 95, 97, 99, 101, 102, 103, 104, 117, 118
Charles Truxton: 41, 44, 46, 57, 58, 67, 81, 82, 88, 115, 123
Mark Wilson: 74

"Out of heaven shall he thunder upon them;
the Lord shall judge *the ends of the earth.*"
1 Samuel 2:10

Published by SIM International Publications

SIM includes Sudan Interior Mission and Andes Evangelical Mission
Australia: P.O. Box 171, Summer Hill, N.S.W. 2130
Canada: 10 Huntingdale Blvd., Scarborough, Ont. M1W 2S5
Great Britain: 84 Beulah Hill, London SE19 3EP, England
New Zealand: P.O. Box 38588, Howick
Singapore: Bras Basah, P.O. Box 239, Singapore 9118
Switzerland: Société Internationale Missionnaire, Rue de Genève 77 bis, 1004 Lausanne
U.S.A.: Cedar Grove, N.J. 07009

Typesetting by Nuprint Services Ltd., Harpenden, Herts
Printed by Garden House Press, London

SIM **BY PRAYER SINCE 1893**